WORD OF MOUTH

CARLTON EDWARDS

AuthorHouse™
1663 Liberty Drive
Bloomington, IN 47403
www.authorhouse.com
Phone: 833-262-8899

Because of the dynamic nature of the Internet, any web addresses or links contained in this book may have changed
since publication and may no longer be valid. The views expressed in this work are solely those of the author and do not
necessarily reflect the views of the publisher, and the publisher hereby disclaims any responsibility for them.

Any people depicted in stock imagery provided by Getty Images are models,
and such images are being used for illustrative purposes only.
Certain stock imagery © Getty Images.

This book is printed on acid-free paper.

ISBN: 978-1-4969-4004-9 (sc)

Print information available on the last page.

Published by AuthorHouse 06/29/2023

authorHOUSE®

First and foremost, I want to thank my wife, Maria Martinez, for all of the support she has given. I also like to thank my daughter Dahiana. Most of the work occurred during the afternoons while my youngest daughter was fighting for my attention. Also at nights, while on vacation, and other times that were inconvenient to my family. My daughter Dayanara, who is five at the time of me finishing this book, has also needed to show patience when her dad was working on Word Of Mouth completion. I want to thank some of my coworkers and friends who kept me inspired as I was writing and getting a feel of the emotions needed to do this book. Most of all, the biggest thanks goes out to Ruby L. for lighting the fire in me to begin the process of writing this book.

#2

As I watch you, I only see my number two
most desired one for the test.
Yes baby, you are the best.
When you make your mark, you leave the
residue of profound blackness.
You pencil, in the essence of your
presence. No one will make
the mistake of saying you were not here,
for no eraser will be needed
to clean up the mess most would
leave behind.
No editor will have to rewrite on
this eight by eleven, for most artists will
only envy your existence of being
the benchmark of woman.

Carlton Edwards

Advice Anyone

Who are you
to give me
advice, your
clothes
are worn and
defiled. Can
good advice
only come
from a well
dressed
person?

Carlton G. Edwards

Borrowed Man New

The True Life Of A Player

I see these men that seem to have it all. They are seen at the best eatery and attend the ritziest balls. Thinking to myself just wishing to be them for one day. Just look at him with that woman, he must have some sort of master plan. Today with her and just yesterday with another, I bet he would even get the mother. With such ease he just dashes about town, I never even saw him with a frown. Oh some say that he has quite the bill. They even say his life is unfulfilled. At the bank he is not allowed. I think with him debt always seems to follow. Time must be drawing near, because he now seems to be running a little scared. Ah I see the big picture now, he does look to be filled with mounting fear. When I am grown and on my own, I will only obtain the things I can afford, for I thirst not to be that BORROWED MAN!

Carlton G. Edwards

4

Busting at the seams

Hey you! You who have me busting at the seams. You who have me floating in a haze, so thick it makes me dizzy. It has become so hard to focus on even the littlest of things because you have me busting at the seams. I wonder if it's real or just a dream, or is it lasting? This question has me lost in my mind. Tell me who are you the one of my dreams for you have me busting at the seams? Will someone just pinch me or kick me. No, not the punch for I'm already out cold on my feet. Yes Miss Lady, you have me busting at the seams. When I look at you I see you as a Queen, knowing that you have me busting at the seams. I have no one to tell of this journey that I seem to be riding. Now I say let me get a grip, for I can not let anyone see me in this state. Now I'm drifting all over the place for I have busted completely out of the seams.

Carlton George Edwards

Castaway Love

Founded on the heap of the castaway lovers, this love I found is the best. I have been alone so long that I was rusty in knowing how to please, I'm a mess. Holding on as tight as possible to the love I found, keeps my feet off the ground. When I see my love I have a puzzled look on my face, who could have castaway such a love? All I can say is finders keepers, losers... losers!

Carlton G. Edwards

Changing of the Season

The morning was a bit crisp,
but thoughts of you would
just warm my planet.
You see the season has just
changed.
I'm just thinking of you and
it brings a fire that burns
inside of me, with flames
as hot as the most
ferocious volcano lava. With
your magma pouring down
my hills, and yes
warming my chills!
I look across the skies and
just dreaming of the day
when our eyes will meet
again.

Every star I see
just brings back a
vision of you,
the most wonderful
flavor to be called woman;
to ever be tasted! I just
want to leave this
mountain top, with my
tongue dripping with the
flavor: that made
the leaves change,
the night come, and the
snow fall.
A thunder just clap, and a
bolt of lightening just flash
across the skies. Yes the
season has changed.

Carlton George Edwards

7

Controlling My Dreams

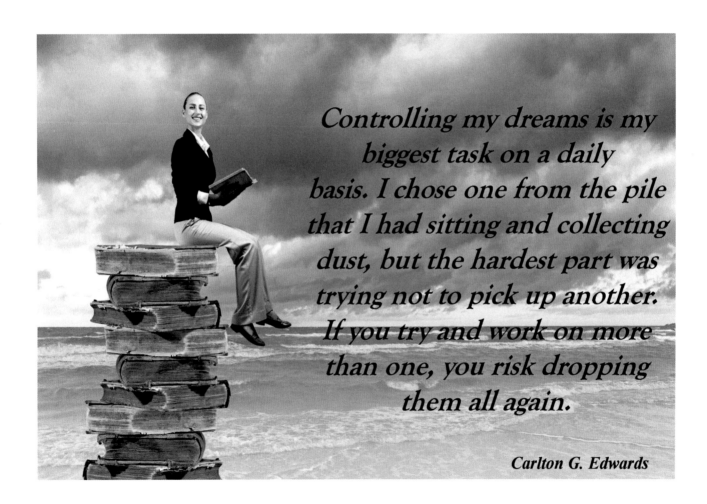

Controlling my dreams is my biggest task on a daily basis. I chose one from the pile that I had sitting and collecting dust, but the hardest part was trying not to pick up another. If you try and work on more than one, you risk dropping them all again.

Carlton G. Edwards

Coping

Consider yourself blessed if the thoughts in your head you can control. There are so many that have a tougher time with the daily keeping it together so as to not let their life just unfold. If I told you my thoughts and you tell me yours, we might see that we all have a mighty task just keeping it together. I know sometimes we may say, why do I think like this? You see, this is the true test of life. We have to pretend as if these thoughts are not there, so things don't go amiss. Some people have it extremely bad and need medication. Remember that the people you see and admire could be dealing with that dreaded affliction.

Carlton G. Edwards

Cyborg Lovers

Is lasting love fading in our society? The future of love may soon only exist with cyborg lovers. We humans seek love only to abandon it when the work to keep it gets hard. Our borgs will be here as visual reminders, showing us the things we have given up on in our society. Carlton G. Edwards

Dream Makers

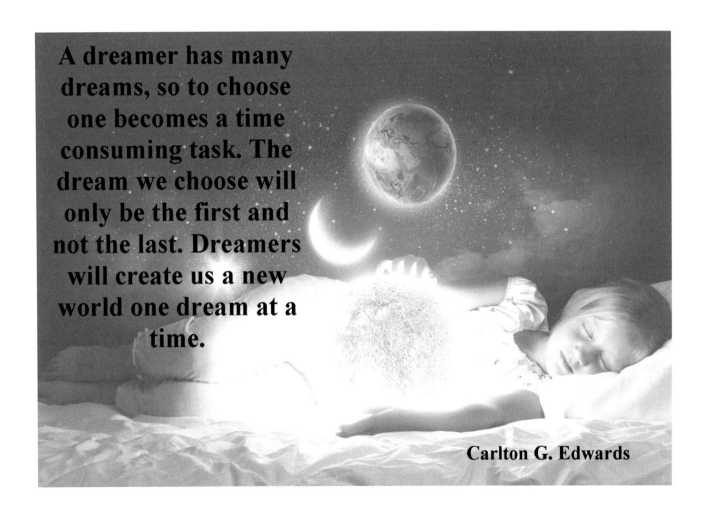

A dreamer has many dreams, so to choose one becomes a time consuming task. The dream we choose will only be the first and not the last. Dreamers will create us a new world one dream at a time.

Carlton G. Edwards

Dream Takers

In the lands of resources and wealth to be
gotten, lies a hand that will kill most dreams.
It will come in the middle of our lives and
divide us all. I woke up with dreams, but went
to sleep with none.

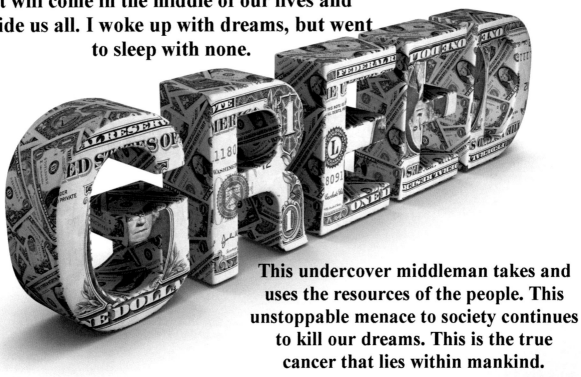

This undercover middleman takes and
uses the resources of the people. This
unstoppable menace to society continues
to kill our dreams. This is the true
cancer that lies within mankind.

Carlton G. Edwards

Dream Walkers

A dream will show you a door, but you must walk through it to reveal its true worth.

Carlton G. Edwards

Extinction By Wars

Not by disease or accident, the extinction of mankind will not be a mystery. Our eyes are open to the fact that men are their own worst enemy. Learning from the mistake that is made do not seems to apply to human conflicts. We have countless skirmishes or wars that have been around for years to centuries. The communication between the factions just don't seem to get any better. We are self-proclaimed to be the smarter being on the planet. I'm lost with the notion that we can take a life in the name of religion. Now, we develop new technologies day by day yet we are still lost with each other. We fight our wars as well as the one of the forefathers, in the name of our kids. Please men when you are done, leave the planet for the animals who once had the run of the place.

Carlton G. Edwards

Faceless Man

When Hello Works

It seems like life gets us all down sometimes. But we cannot become that faceless man. Let's not walk around with a frown on our face. I know that is not what we want to project. So if you see that faceless man say "hello," or "how are you doing?"You never know you might just give him a new face. The tear drops and frown needs to be wiped away and turn upside down.

Carlton G. Edwards

Family Glue

As the head of the house I will hold this family together no matter what it takes. Looking to the left, looking to the right, my family is going all over the place tonight. I will guide them and make sure they are safe, I just can't afford to make any mistakes. I'm called the head or the man of the house, but I am still trying to impress my spouse. I will not rest until everyone is asleep or all are safely in the house.

Carlton G. Edwards

Free All Women

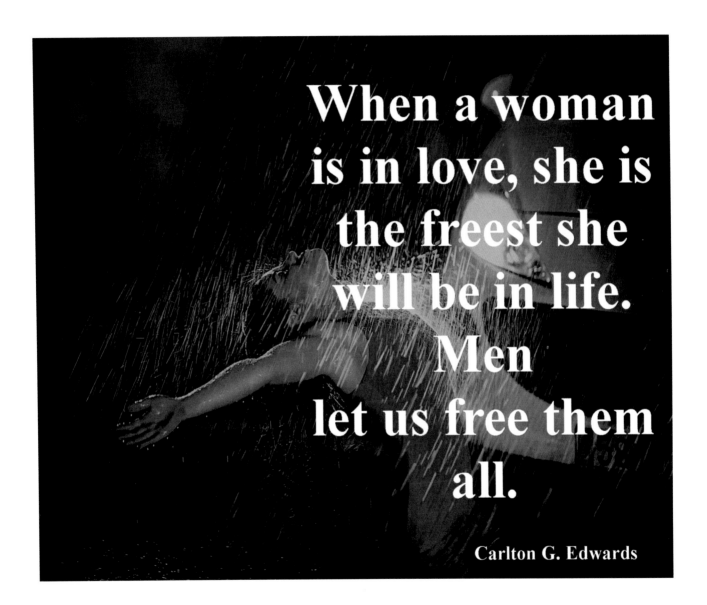

When a woman is in love, she is the freest she will be in life. Men let us free them all.

Carlton G. Edwards

Friendship And Marriage

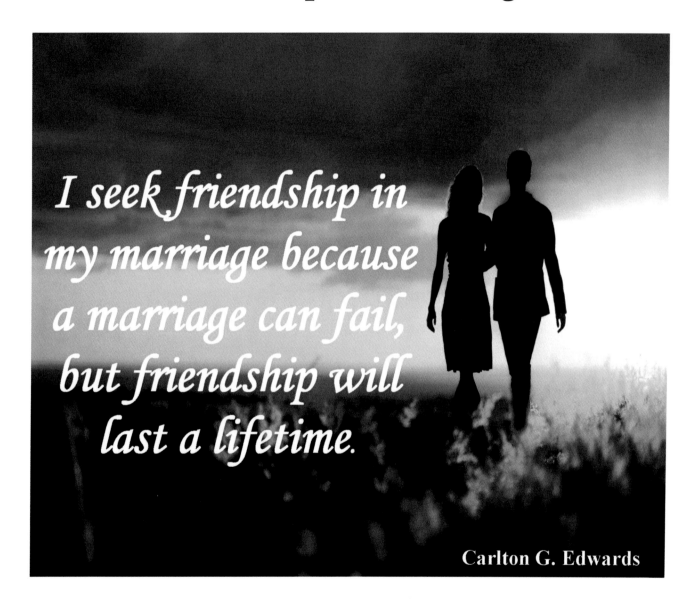

I seek friendship in my marriage because a marriage can fail, but friendship will last a lifetime.

Carlton G. Edwards

Ghostly Thoughts

A bright idea is best used when you are living.

Carlton G. Edwards

Good or Bad War

To foreign lands they were sent to fight for reasons not quite understood. The giving of lives and limbs, some were brought back in a box made of wood. Ribbons are hung and tears are shed, for in unknown lands our soldiers bleed. This war just goes on and on with no end in sight. Spending holidays, birthdays, anniversaries' just countless days and nights. They were told to fight with pride for the old RED, WHITE and BLUE, but only one color stands out when looking at all the bodies and that one bloodied shoe. They are now leaving behind single parent families and babies unseen. The broken hearts of mothers, fathers, wives and husbands and a nation asking why or what is it all about? The value of the dollar has hit record low; the knocking on another door saying "son it's your time to go." Scratching his head wondering what to do while packing, but wanting to say do I have to go. The cycle continues sending more to war but bringing back less and less. The ones that come back all together or not, are left a mess and sometimes not even blessed!

CARLTON G. EDWARDS

20

Good Woman Please

The tender touch of a woman is none
so great as to when you are down.
Having a woman that is there for you
when you are up or down, makes
the challenges of life an easier road to
travel. A good woman is hard to find
because once taken they are never
given up. If you see a good woman
that is not taken, don't blink she will
be gone that fast.

Carlton G. Edwards

Hello Anybody Out There

I NEED YOU AND YOU

What have we done? Not wanting to talk to you and you. Can we now make it with just ourselves on this earth? I closed my eyes and with me alone in a place where there was no one but me. I just smiled and say thank you. This is why I wanted to be left alone, or so I thought. As my day started I walked from here to there and no one in sight. With a smile on my face I began to sing. I sang for hours and with each hour I felt like the greatest singer alive. Then I realized that no one told me I sounded great, but that's ok... I was by myself. I was a little tired so I sat down and started to talk to ...Oh, Myself. Feeling the pain of hunger creeping up on me, but that did not matter for you see by now I know food was not the first thing on my mind. Without you here there is no me, so I apologize because I need you and you!

CARLTON G EDWARDS

Hello World

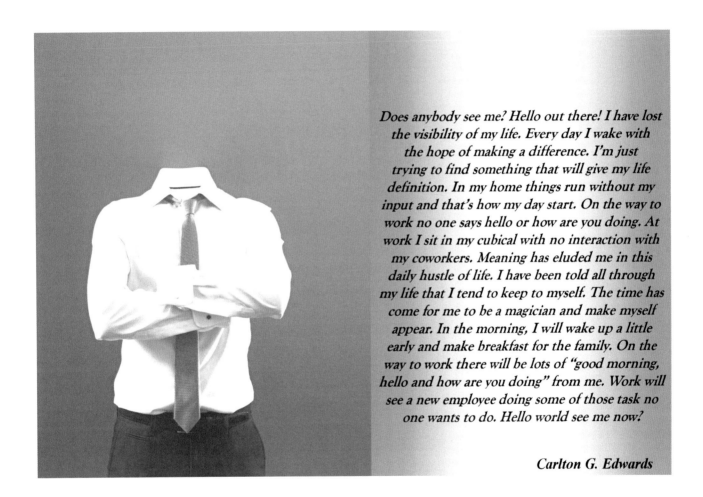

Does anybody see me? Hello out there! I have lost the visibility of my life. Every day I wake with the hope of making a difference. I'm just trying to find something that will give my life definition. In my home things run without my input and that's how my day start. On the way to work no one says hello or how are you doing. At work I sit in my cubical with no interaction with my coworkers. Meaning has eluded me in this daily hustle of life. I have been told all through my life that I tend to keep to myself. The time has come for me to be a magician and make myself appear. In the morning, I will wake up a little early and make breakfast for the family. On the way to work there will be lots of "good morning, hello and how are you doing" from me. Work will see a new employee doing some of those task no one wants to do. Hello world see me now?

Carlton G. Edwards

Holiday Time

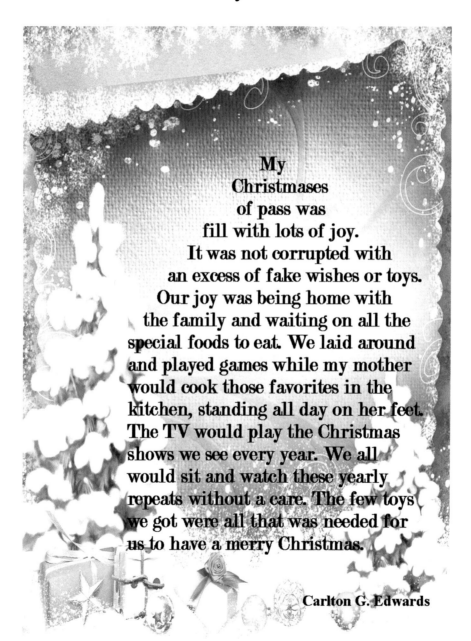

My
Christmases
of pass was
fill with lots of joy.
It was not corrupted with
an excess of fake wishes or toys.
Our joy was being home with
the family and waiting on all the
special foods to eat. We laid around
and played games while my mother
would cook those favorites in the
kitchen, standing all day on her feet.
The TV would play the Christmas
shows we see every year. We all
would sit and watch these yearly
repeats without a care. The few toys
we got were all that was needed for
us to have a merry Christmas.

Carlton G. Edwards

In Your Custody

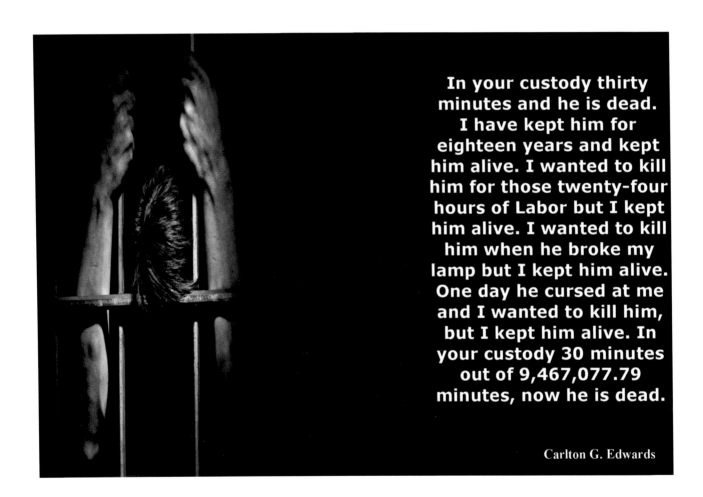

In your custody thirty minutes and he is dead. I have kept him for eighteen years and kept him alive. I wanted to kill him for those twenty-four hours of Labor but I kept him alive. I wanted to kill him when he broke my lamp but I kept him alive. One day he cursed at me and I wanted to kill him, but I kept him alive. In your custody 30 minutes out of 9,467,077.79 minutes, now he is dead.

Carlton G. Edwards

It's your Choice

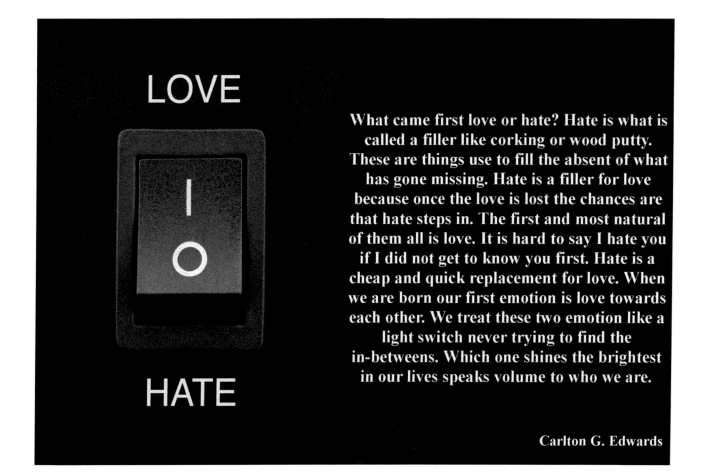

LOVE

HATE

What came first love or hate? Hate is what is called a filler like corking or wood putty. These are things use to fill the absent of what has gone missing. Hate is a filler for love because once the love is lost the chances are that hate steps in. The first and most natural of them all is love. It is hard to say I hate you if I did not get to know you first. Hate is a cheap and quick replacement for love. When we are born our first emotion is love towards each other. We treat these two emotion like a light switch never trying to find the in-betweens. Which one shines the brightest in our lives speaks volume to who we are.

Carlton G. Edwards

Label Them Dead

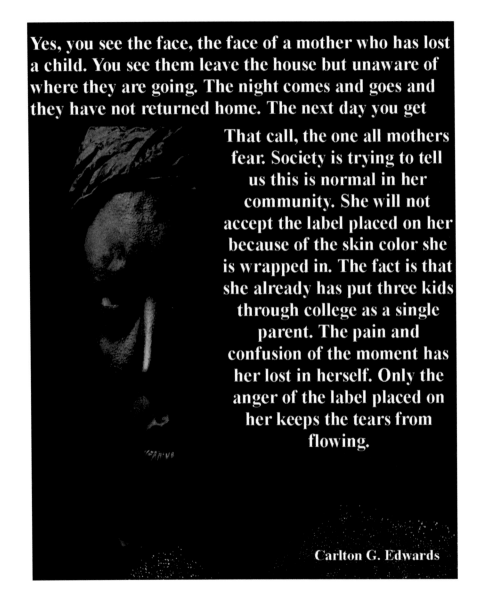

Yes, you see the face, the face of a mother who has lost a child. You see them leave the house but unaware of where they are going. The night comes and goes and they have not returned home. The next day you get

That call, the one all mothers fear. Society is trying to tell us this is normal in her community. She will not accept the label placed on her because of the skin color she is wrapped in. The fact is that she already has put three kids through college as a single parent. The pain and confusion of the moment has her lost in herself. Only the anger of the label placed on her keeps the tears from flowing.

Carlton G. Edwards

Legs Of Pine

As she walks in the room with legs as tall as Georgia pine, my eyes would roam catching her. Her arms are looking strong, firm and steady as the branches on that tall wintry Longleaf. She smells fresh as the greenery of the outdoors in the spring time. Leaning on the bar, her hair is as thick and strong looking like the prickly needle of the pitch pine. I'm getting closer so I can offer her a glass of this aged fine wine. I am the one they call dogwood, the old tree. This cross breeding would be difficult for most botany enthuses to understand. I can envision us with little off shoots in the coming spring, just baffling the minds of the horticulturist that would pass this way looking for rare finds. So until we can rub trunks together, let me grab some sun so I can continue to grow until our branches meet. Now look at the wood that Georgia pine has created in my trunks! Soon we will have our very own little pinecones.

Carlton G. Edwards

Life A Grain Of Sand

In the youth of my life I seem to be a grain of sand on top of the heap of the hour glass. Never stopping to glance at the bottom droppers for fear never entered my mind as I swirled through life. Now mid glance I think back of the drifts I once laid atop of. Survival seems to be the thought of the day now. I now can see the funnel of the back half of my swirling life. All of my dreams fulfilled or not, seem to be a daily reflection. Not wanting to make a bad turn at this point drives me to a never ending view of the good or bad happenings of the day. I dare not miss a beat or my fate will be near, for the neck of the drop off point grows closer with every turn. I give myself a shot of hope knowing that I have so many things yet to be done, so I think of the high points. My bag of wisdom is still filled with joy and up turns to stay afloat. So as the sand of life twirls about me, I am the rock of slate needing to find a mate to glass over my life. It now seems to be blowing by so fast and knowing these are the window years that need to be protected with a tint, from the plight of life's unpredictabilities.

Carlton G. Edwards

29

Lock and Key

Bringing back some of the things of the past, just to protect your most prized possession. This is not to negate the trust you have but just to satisfy your obsession. I know how you feel wanting to keep all you have yours and finding ways to make sure. When you are away and are no longer in sight. Keep it under lock and key because this winter will have lots of cold nights.

Carlton G. Edwards

Love Foundation

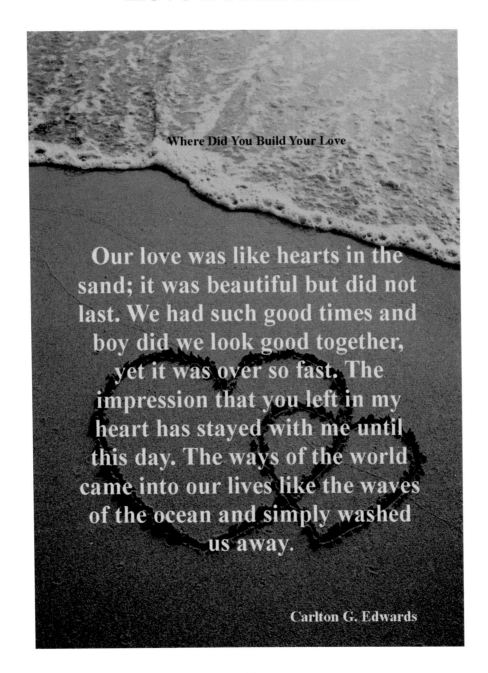

Where Did You Build Your Love

Our love was like hearts in the sand; it was beautiful but did not last. We had such good times and boy did we look good together, yet it was over so fast. The impression that you left in my heart has stayed with me until this day. The ways of the world came into our lives like the waves of the ocean and simply washed us away.

Carlton G. Edwards

Love In Excess

Your love is like the wet dewy drops in the rain forest of love. I could only handle but one drop, so the banks of my heart will not overflow or succumb with the deluge of you. I hoarded all the vases of my land to pour the excess of your love. Your beauty will be that one stem of rose in each of the vase that I possess.

Carlton G. Edwards

Man Tissue

Seeing you cry makes me feel cloudy inside. Wanting to wipe your eyes with my heart to let you know I feel your pain. I know not what caused the pain but I will try to be your man tissue. Life brings us happiness and pain but we sometime need someone to be the blotter that dries the tears from our eyes. Who am I to you? Who you are to me does not matter, for seeing my friend in pain leaves me apart from my own troubles. I only want to put a smile on your face this moment knowing that whatever it is will take time to go on its way, so you can have the brighter day that you deserve. So I say wipe away the tears with me your man tissue and together we will solve this so call bitter issue. Now one, two three blow the nose and dry the tears and yes smile. Man tissue must go now and dry some other tears away, SMILE!

Carlton G Edwards

Memories of You 2

I will always remember you the silent but strong partner of mine. The years we shared from one to fifty or until the end of time. You gave me many fulfilled seasons of which I keep and cherish every day. You are no longer with me in these rooms of the house we shared, but still talking to me as if you were just a whisper away. Our kids now all grown and with families of their own, only remind me of the life we gave to them to be passed on for generations to come. As I lay here in the bed and talk to you every night, lets me know we still belong together because for your love I still succumb. Until tomorrow when we speak again you strong Masonic man. I keep thoughts of us when we first walked holding hand in hand. Turning out the lights, closing my eyes and when I awake to embark on another day I will keep you close to me in mind, spirit, body and soul, IN GOD I say AMEN!

Carlton G. Edwards

Missing Valentine

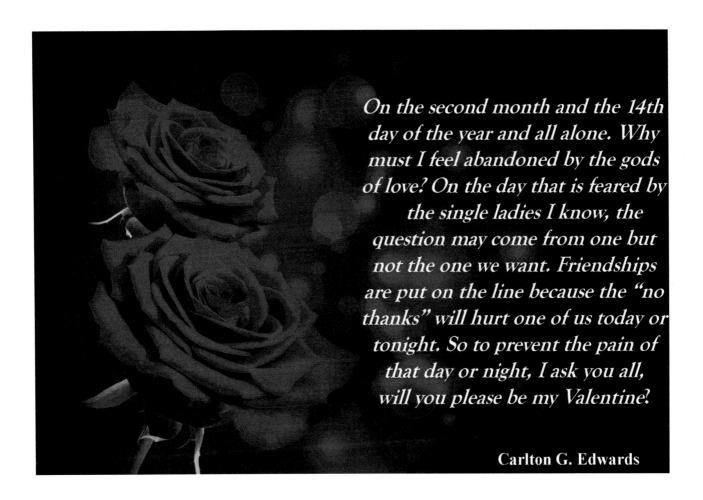

On the second month and the 14th day of the year and all alone. Why must I feel abandoned by the gods of love? On the day that is feared by the single ladies I know, the question may come from one but not the one we want. Friendships are put on the line because the "no thanks" will hurt one of us today or tonight. So to prevent the pain of that day or night, I ask you all, will you please be my Valentine?

Carlton G. Edwards

Misting You 2

Looking outside, seeing the
mist
coming down, I would say
that it is misting.
Wanting you here next to me
lets me know that I am
misting you.
It has become so hard just to
look a the world without
thinking of you, so I
know that
I am misting you.
I walked outside looking up as
the mist falls in my face, and
tasting the fine mist hitting
my tongue, yeah I'm
misting you.
A fog just rolled in carrying
the very essence of you, the
misty one.
This only solidifies the fact
that I have become engulfed
in the
misty fog of you.
Somebody better grab me
because this brother has gone
googly eyes for you.
Short and sweet, just
misting you.

Carlton George Edwards

Mother Of Life

She is the one with the two hearts beating inside. Let's celebrate her for all the gifts she brings to mankind. Without these gifts we would cease to exist. When you see a woman with two or more hearts, remember her worth and let her know it.

Carlton G. Edwards

My Coma

Finding myself just drifting away; with thoughts of my childhood consuming me. All of the dreams I had as a child are fresh in my mind. I can smell the dinner my mother is cooking and can't wait to eat. What is this state I'm in? It feels so strange because I want to go in the house but don't seem to be able to move. I will just stay here and wait until my mother call me. If she doesn't hear from me she will come and get me.

Carlton G. Edwards

My Frozen Valentine

I'm here on the bridge where I first met my new love. I brought all that was needed to celebrate our first valentine. The time is near for my love to arrive so I opened the wine trying to keep warm from the chill in the air. The time seems to be going by minutes then hours and an empty bottle of wine later. As cold and drunk as I'm mad, I decide to leave. Just at that point I see my love approaching and I just lit up like a Christmas tree. He explained his delay and offer to warm my cold and shivering body.

Carlton G. Edwards

My Inside Face

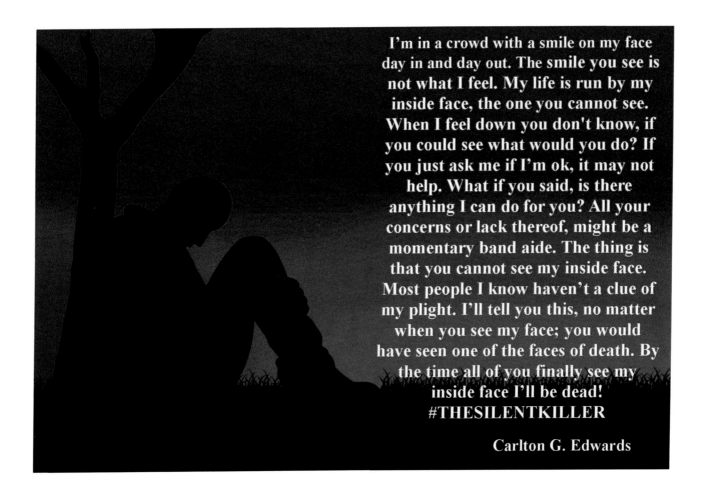

I'm in a crowd with a smile on my face day in and day out. The smile you see is not what I feel. My life is run by my inside face, the one you cannot see. When I feel down you don't know, if you could see what would you do? If you just ask me if I'm ok, it may not help. What if you said, is there anything I can do for you? All your concerns or lack thereof, might be a momentary band aide. The thing is that you cannot see my inside face. Most people I know haven't a clue of my plight. I'll tell you this, no matter when you see my face; you would have seen one of the faces of death. By the time all of you finally see my inside face I'll be dead!
#THESILENTKILLER

Carlton G. Edwards

My Stupid Cupid

Jilted by the love gods who sent me a cupid that should have been retired. Every time he drew back his bow I got someone unemployed or recently fired. Tonight is the night I need for him to get it right. I have waited for a while for this day 2/14, please send someone that's out of sight. I hope that my expectations are not too high on this day. There is a knock on the door and my hopes are running on high, let's hope I don't have to send them far, far away. Looking through the peep hole as my suspense takes over, o no what a sight I can just cry, his name must be Rover. Cupid I'm done with you! You sent me someone from the other holiday, the one that you say booooo. To the gods of love please send me another cupid. For this one is the one we all call stupid.

Carlton G. Edwards

41

Nomad Dreams

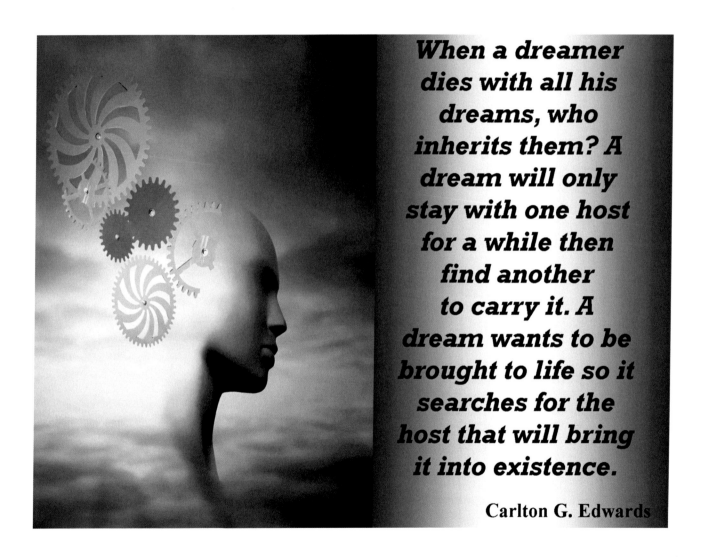

When a dreamer dies with all his dreams, who inherits them? A dream will only stay with one host for a while then find another to carry it. A dream wants to be brought to life so it searches for the host that will bring it into existence.

Carlton G. Edwards

Now You Call Me Old Shoes

You tossed me away despite all that we have been
through. Maybe I am not as shiny and round or
thick at the bottom as I used to be. You used to
wear me to all of your affairs. Now you toss me
aside not wanting to be seen with me anymore.
You just spit on me instead of applying the polish
you once used all over me. I should have seen this
coming, my friends told me of your habits. I
don't know what you will be slipping into next.
You may try and squeeze into any old thing I see.
One of these days you may get some sort of growth
from that new habit. I can only hope I can be
rebuild again and get someone who will get
pleasure in sticking the right fit inside of me some
day. Then I will be seen out and about with a new
shine on me. I hear talks about you having
switching sides 'on the down low.' Well, I don't
want to think like that, but if you did, please make
it "Stiletthoes." ha ha... Stiletthoes of the street
walkers, the ones at night on the corners. I think
you know what I mean. If you by accident should
slip into me in the dark one night, I can say it was
good while it lasted. I will click my heels in hope of
that night.

Carlton G Edwards

43

Old Saint Nick

You knew Old Saint Nick was
getting old and losing his grip.
The way he used to dodge, duck
and hide, down chimneys
he would slide.
He would hook up the sleigh and
ride through the night,
of him no guard dog could
get a bite.
Now up in years and not as
quick on his feet,
even the littlest of guard dogs
will bite chunks of meat.
There are no more Prancer or
Rudolph, all the reindeers
have retired in Miami
and are now playing golf.
Our gifts are now delivered
by the local mail or UPS.
We can only remember the past
and say, O what a MESS.

Dear Santa
Carlton Edwards

One of these Days

One of these days maybe I'll understand our meeting.

One of these days I'll understand you.

One of these days I'll understand what I feel for you.

One of these days I'll tell you all my dreams.

One of these days you will understand me.

One of these days all of this will make sense.

One of these days might never come, but this day I

know I miss you.

Carlton G. Edwards

Pillow Talk

I cried my tears
throughout the night; with
no one to hear, just holding
my pillow tight.
Feeling the pain of the love I
have lost,
now I know what runs my
world or who is
the boss.
I know now the price I paid
for the feelings I shared.
Now I'm wondering if and
when I will ever give my
feelings again or just run
scared.

Carlton G. Edwards

Playing House

This is a relationship with no strings attached or so we said to each other. We spent the better part of three years seeing each other when time permitted. Then one day out of the blue she asked, where is this thing of ours going? I knew all along that she would not be my one, so now I owe her the truth. You can play house but eventually the house begins to feel like home for someone.

Carlton G. Edwards

Pockets of Time

Always Fleeting

Pockets of time seem to be with us from the moment we were born until the day that we pass. We try to hold on to some of it from time to time, trying not to let go of it in fear that is won't last. But time is what we all cherish when reflecting on the good or bad, it will take us from happy to sad. The times we spend with family and friends at work rest or play, will stay with us for the rest of our days. We keep these little pockets of times with us without a choice. Then, there comes a time when we are sitting, laying, and walking, it comes to us like a vision or a voice. We sometimes will close our eyes just to go to one of those special times trying to keep the strength to move on. Now that is why we will always keep these little pockets of time.

Carlton G. Edwards

Ruby

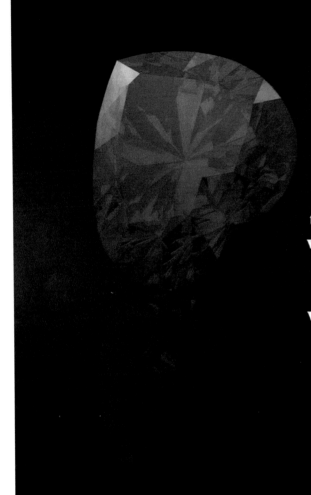

The one that is so often feared as well as
admired and also can make you as red as a beat, walking away and stomping your feet. Then will send you laughs via the net which makes us wonder, can this Ruby also be sweet? We are baffled knowing love travel in many forms and colors. Not wanting to be misled, we only wonder and stare at the
brilliance of the Ruby red. We will work this gem in the rough but trying not to let it all get in our head. Yes, that ruby that have been mined for years on end, should be admired from a far because the expense of rubbing that Ruby to brilliance comes at a heighten price. A gem to some and birthstone to

Carlton G. Edwards

Secret Love

You are the woman of my dreams.
the one I have love for that is unforeseen.
If I have not said this today, maybe my
mind was lead astray.
You have a grip on me that
is stronger than glue, so woman I say
I LOVE YOU.
I know you are the bride of another,
and mother of his broods, to them I could
not be rude. So I accept my place in this
mess ,and only with these words I can
get it off my chest.
I will respect the situation at hand,
for only with god's grace there
can be any other plan.
I know what I'm about to say
is nothing new, so again I say, I love you!

Carlton G. Edwards

Silent Life

My silence is not for sale because she is a woman and my friend. She doesn't have the courage to tell of the hell behind the walls of her life, but I see she can't fend. We cannot as humans keep silent to the domestic violence abuse we see. There is a family member that is caught in this daily wrong of being beating down to their hands and knees. I haven't the understanding of this behavior because I look at females as a gift to mankind. The thing for most men is that a good mate is so hard to find. The actions of a few have placed our search in a situation of doubt with our prospects. To all the abusers please get a grip on your life and give up the girlfriend and the wife if for them you can't respect. #IAMTELLING

Carlton G. Edwards

51

Skeleton Keys

The day came when we exchanged our keys.
Still not thinking it's the time for me to drop
on left, right, or both knees. Waiting to see where
this time of bliss will take us; still in fear of our
first real fuss. We walked around, talked about, ate
in and out, but the air lingers with feelings of doubt.
My door would open so would hers, using these newly
traded keys. In each other places, me standing she sitting,
we would even see each other take well deserved pees.
Then days became weeks, months and years and together
we cried some tears. Saying the I DOs have come and gone,
along with kids for whom we both cared. Now in years of
our passing no longer in flesh or skeleton bones. Only the
dust left behind like dried rotten leaves. Our spirits looking
back knowing we swapped the right keys, the one that would
unlock the door to each other souls. Lurking now in spirit and
reflecting back with ghostly smiles; yes we are pleased for the
swapping of our keys.

Carlton G. Edwards

Smile Smiles Smiling

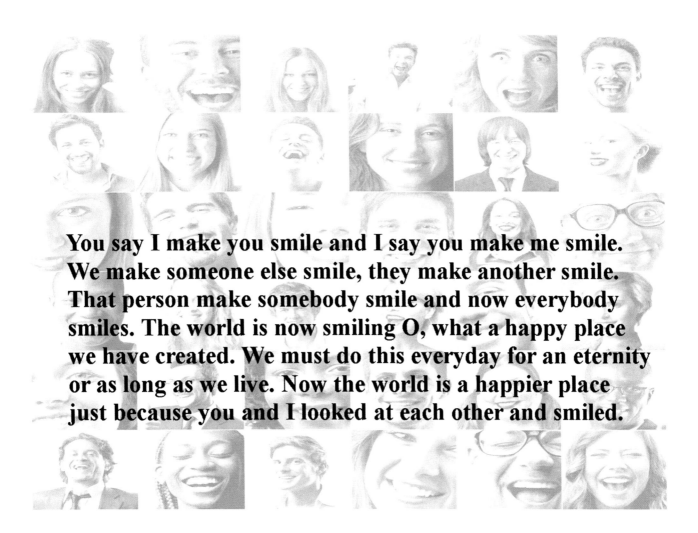

You say I make you smile and I say you make me smile. We make someone else smile, they make another smile. That person make somebody smile and now everybody smiles. The world is now smiling O, what a happy place we have created. We must do this everyday for an eternity or as long as we live. Now the world is a happier place just because you and I looked at each other and smiled.

Snow Angels

Winters passed, flashes in my mind of this day. Just walking and thinking of the beauty of snow just falling. As I walked in the open field with the white magic all around me and on everything. Suddenly I was caught by surprise, someone on their back lying in the snow and flapping their arms. As I approached I can now see that it was a woman. When close enough to her to see a face sprinkled with white speckles, she said, "how do you like my angels?" Not knowing what to say the words "You are an angel" crossed my lips. She only smiled and then stood up saying thanks. At this point I am astonished to hear the response of which I did not expect. Now beginning to walk side by side and talking about things I do not remember because I simply drifted into dreamland. We must have walked for hours or so it seemed. I remember seeing the snow rise inch by inch. The time came that day when she said so long. It was like a cloud has just covered my day and then at this point I realized that all snow angels must melt.

Carlton George Edwards

Strength to you my Queen

If all I can offer is strength to
you my queen, then so be it. For
the work ahead is as hard as is
the rough road,
but there is light on the
horizon. This world of ours has
many holes to patch and new
ventures to seek, but what is
needed is the strength that lies
within.
As I look at the sky and pray to
the higher power, I ask that he
give us the strength to hold on.
For this was not by chance that
our worlds crossed in this
universe.
My queen you will have the test
of time to work
the fields of life, for only with
that work does the fruit of the
future bears prosperity so
STRENGTH TO YOU MY
QUEEN!

Carlton Edwards

Subway Affair

Walking on air and seemingly having no fear. I'm floating so high without wings or care. There could be no wrong and it feels so sweet. Every day when I see her I'm swept off my feet. In my mind thoughts of us together and thinking that we belong. Standing in the same car, all control of my mind slipping away and then gone. Now I'm hoping that this ride can somehow be prolonged. I'm just floating from thought to thought, now hearing the beating of my heart with the rhythm of a Jamaican pushcart. Reality slaps me in the face when it's time for us to go our separate ways. Next stop 17th and Broad or is it Main? Well, until tomorrow when I ride this line holding out hope this feeling will be the same.

Carlton G. Edwards

The Fork In The Road

There will always be that fork in the road of life. We approach them as we make our way through the day. We make a decision which way to go. Not knowing if it is the right choice, but without missing a beat onward in our life step by step we go. With the tools in hand from pass choices we carry the knowledge we think we need for that point and time. Sometimes with the pronounce beating of our hearts and with bit of fear and feeling of weaken knees another step we take moving ourselves. Each day the old choices have more strength than the previous day. These old and new decisions give us the confidence along with queasy feelings, but ahhh we go on. That fork in the road of life will be there today, tomorrow and the day after for the rest of our lives, but it's good, so together we will keep moving on for there is another Fork In The Road that lies ahead.

Carlton G. Edwards

The Wind Beneath Me

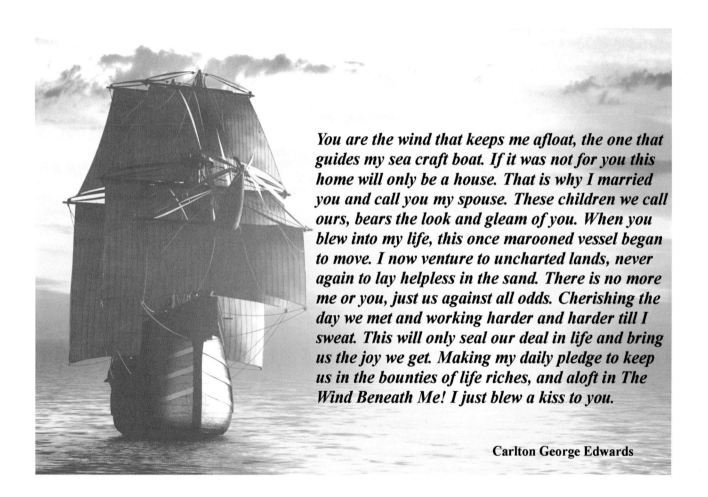

You are the wind that keeps me afloat, the one that guides my sea craft boat. If it was not for you this home will only be a house. That is why I married you and call you my spouse. These children we call ours, bears the look and gleam of you. When you blew into my life, this once marooned vessel began to move. I now venture to uncharted lands, never again to lay helpless in the sand. There is no more me or you, just us against all odds. Cherishing the day we met and working harder and harder till I sweat. This will only seal our deal in life and bring us the joy we get. Making my daily pledge to keep us in the bounties of life riches, and aloft in The Wind Beneath Me! I just blew a kiss to you.

Carlton George Edwards

Timeless Love

The times we spend are so
precious to me, they need to be bottled and
tossed in the sea.
A thousand years later, opened and wonderful
moments revealed, how stupendous that will be.
For even when these bones
are dried and rotten, our times together will never
be forgotten. You see, it is not in my mind
but my soul that you reside. When the bottle
is opened, then and only then we will be
able to walk side by side.

Carlton G. Edwards

Un-Lynching My Mind

THE NEW PROTEST

I'm in search of the mind I know I should have. The thoughts that others think I should display feel all wrong. Searching for the mind that we know all man was born to have, has become an uphill battle. Having not being taught to think as a man or a leader makes the fight a little tougher. I will find that misplaced mind of mine because I no longer let the world beat me into submitting my god given right to think like a god. There will be no Willie Lynching in this life anymore.

Carlton G. Edwards

Whose Dreams

As a child, all my dreams
were mine.
As a young adult, my
dreams were mine to
fulfill.
As a father, my dreams
began to gather dust.
As a husband, my dreams
began to rust.
Now as a single man, I
will try to dust them off
and get a fresh start.
This is something that I
feel I must. I am so
lost with just me and
them now, not
knowing which way
to go. One thing I must
say, dreams are ours as a
child and as an adult.
Never give them shelf
life too long, for the
day will come when we
say, I should have, could
have, and the blame is
ours to the END!

CHILD

YOUNG
ADULT

HUSBAND

DAD

Carlton George Edwards

Woman Strong

A man could never understand the strength of a woman. If she could give him five of her days to bear, he would love her the way he should.

Carlton G. Edwards

Women of the WWW

Sight Unseen

Given up for dead were my emotions with no place to carry them. My life has become a one way street that seems to lead to a dead end. I walk down the street and see couples holding hands and laughing. Now I'm making haste to go home, for there is only one way for me, surfing the net. Finding love has changed, no more social clubs, bars or night clubs. You now have to be jacked in, plugged up, and reaching out through a hub. Feeling confined to the inside world because out there I see him and him, her and her and boy and girl. So I sit here site unseen and chat to words only on the screen. I have profiles to check and a mouse to click. So WWW@home.com CLICK CLICK!

CARLTON G. EDWARDS

Working My Nerves

I have learned a new language;
I can now talk to a hand. The
first time I saw it, I thought it
meant stop so I did. Now I'm
confused, so then my question
is, why do you keep raising
that hand at me? She
answered, "please, you just be
working my nerves!" I need to
know when I am working her
nerve because everything I do
is "working her nerves."

Carlton G. Edwards

Printed in the United States
by Baker & Taylor Publisher Services